EXPLORERS AND PATHFINDERS

DON QUINLAN

CANADA

A PEOPLE'S HISTORY

FITZHENRY & WHITESIDE

Explorers and Pathfinders © 2004 Fitzhenry & Whiteside

National Library of Canada Cataloguing in Publication

Quinlan, Don, 1947-
    Explorers and pathfinders / Don Quinlan.

(Canada: a people's history)
Includes bibliographical references and index.
ISBN 1-55041-444-5

    1. Canada—Discovery and exploration—Juvenile literature.
2. Explorers—Canada—Biography—Juvenile literature.
I. Title. II. Title: Explorers and pathfinders.
III. Series: Canada: a people's history (Markham, Ont.)

FC172.Q55 2003   j971.01   C2003-903435-6

All inquiries should be addressed to: In the United States:
Fitzhenry & Whiteside Limited   121 Harvard Avenue, Suite 2
195 Allstate Parkway,   Allston, Massachusetts 02134
Markham, Ontario   L3R 4T8

www.fitzhenry.ca   godwit@fitzhenry.ca

Fitzhenry & Whiteside acknowledge with thanks the Canada Council for the Arts, the Government of Canada through its Book Publishing Industry Development Program, and the Ontario Arts Council for their support in our publishing Program.

Fitzhenry & Whiteside are grateful to the Canadian Broadcasting Corporation for their assistance in the preparation of this volume in the book series based on their 17-episode, bilingual television documentary series, *Canada: A People's History*. For more information about *Canada: A People's History*, please visit **www.cbc.ca/history**.
Canada: A People's History © 2000, 2001 Canadian Broadcasting Corporation

Book Credits:
Series Consultants: Donald Bogle, Don Quinlan
Project Manager: Doug Panasis, resources.too
Senior Editor: Susan Petersiel Berg
Photo Researcher: Lisa Brant
Copy Editor/Indexer: Penny Hozy
Layout and Designer: Darrell McCalla

Canadian Broadcasting Corporation Credits:
CBC Representative: Karen Bower

Printed and bound in Canada.
1 2 3 4 5   07 06 05 04 03

Contents

INTRODUCTION

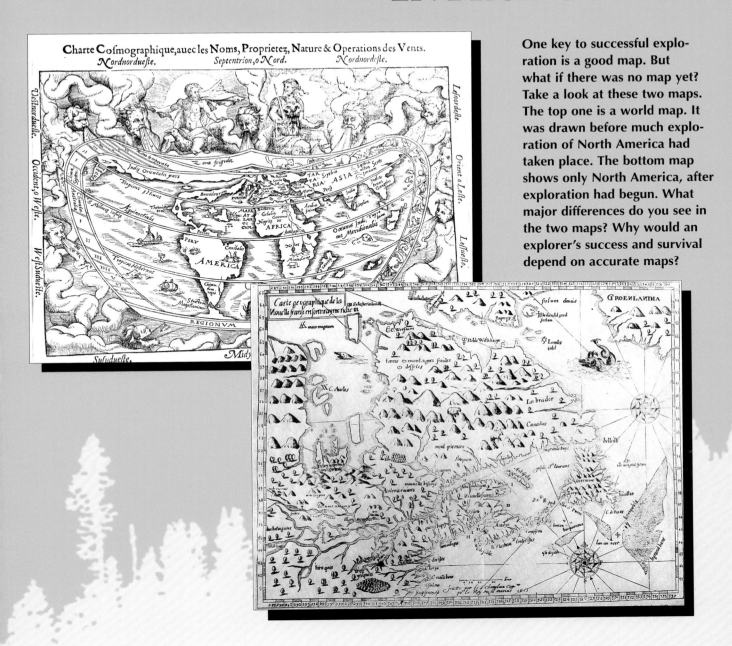

One key to successful exploration is a good map. But what if there was no map yet? Take a look at these two maps. The top one is a world map. It was drawn before much exploration of North America had taken place. The bottom map shows only North America, after exploration had begun. What major differences do you see in the two maps? Why would an explorer's success and survival depend on accurate maps?

THE BIG IDEA

Exploration has shaped the history of Canada. When the Europeans first came here, they knew nothing about the land. They were guided in their explorations by the First Nations peoples who already lived here. Fishers explored the coasts, fur traders pushed into the interior and across the land, and settlers came to farm. French traders had children with Aboriginal women and the Métis nation was born. French, English, First Nations, Métis – all clashed and battled until they had forged the nation we know today.

TIMELINE

1492 Columbus reaches the Americas.

1500 Corte-Real explores Newfoundland and Labrador coastlines.

1524 Verazzano sails and maps 3000 km of North America's eastern coastline.

1534 Jacques Cartier's first voyage.

1541–43 Cartier and Roberval fail to establish a permanent colony in North America.

1497 Cabot lands in Newfoundland.

1520 Fagundes succeeds in building a colony on Cape Breton.

1526 Allyon reaches the Atlantic Coast.

1535 Cartier enters St. Lawrence and winters near Stadacona.

Jacques Cartier

Fear of the unknown made many people's imaginations run wild in the early days of exploration. Most ocean-going ships were pretty small by today's standards. Storms and winds and whales terrified some mariners. Many ships never returned, and people invented amazing stories for their disappearances. Early mapmakers wrote "Here be dragons" to show unexplored regions on their maps. If you believed that dragons and sea creatures were real, would you sail into the waters where they lived?

PICTURE THIS

Can you imagine being asked to go on a long, dangerous journey to an unknown place? What if you had no idea how long or how dangerous this trip might be? What if you didn't know where you were going or what you would find there? What if your fellow travellers were dangerous criminals who were violent and unpredictable? What if the vehicle that you travelled in was small, cramped, and not very well built? Think about the people already living in the lands you plan to explore: how would they feel about your arrival?

TIMELINE

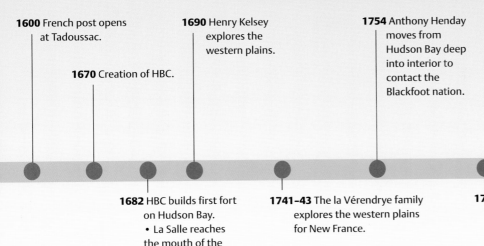

1600 French post opens at Tadoussac.

1670 Creation of HBC.

1682 HBC builds first fort on Hudson Bay.
• La Salle reaches the mouth of the Mississippi River.

1690 Henry Kelsey explores the western plains.

1741–43 The la Vérendrye family explores the western plains for New France.

1754 Anthony Henday moves from Hudson Bay deep into interior to contact the Blackfoot nation.

1759 Battle of Quebec.

1763 Quebec is given to Great Britain.

Imagine hearing stories of explorers falling off the world or being eaten by terrifying creatures. Think about being gone, and away from your family and friends, for many months or many years. Think about the other people taking similar journeys who might try to harm, capture, or even kill you.

So, do you still want to go on this journey?

These questions and thoughts would make most people think twice about exploration in a new land. There aren't too many Canadians today who would choose to do something so impossible and so likely to end in failure. Yet in the first centuries of Canada's history, many people were willing to risk everything to pursue the unknown. If these explorers had not taken such incredible risks, Canada might never have been explored, or become the nation it is today. Risk, excitement, danger, defeat, and victory are threads in the fabric of Canada's history. Some who explored were heroes, others were villains. Some experienced great success, some experienced great failure, many experienced great tragedy. Those who already lived on Canada's land experienced success and tragedy, too. All of their stories have helped to create our story, the history of Canada's people.

SETTING THE SCENE

The First Nations in North America

When you examine history, you may find that people use the word "discover" when they describe European explorers coming to North America. But none of these explorers discovered anything. All of the regions that they were seeing for the first time

The Cost of Exploration

Travelling across oceans, plunging deep into wilderness and surviving the harsh Canadian winter made exploration expensive as well as dangerous. Few explorers had all the equipment they needed. Sometimes they lost their supplies in an ocean gale or crashing rapids. Sometimes they simply ran out, having grossly miscalculated what they would need. There were human costs, too. Exploration usually meant conflict — with other explorers, with the people inhabiting the land, with fellow expedition members. These conflicts often led to rivalry, violence, and all-out war.

TIMELINE

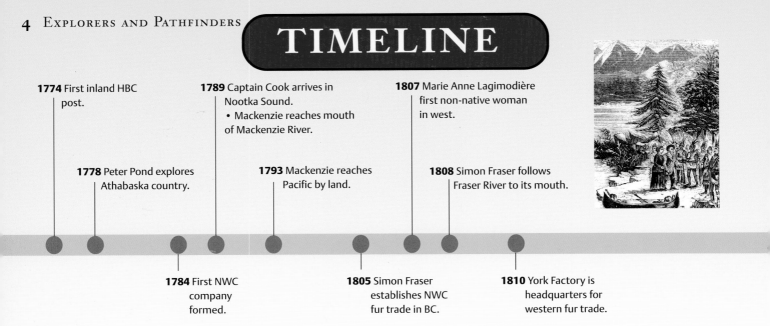

1774 First inland HBC post.

1778 Peter Pond explores Athabaska country.

1784 First NWC company formed.

1789 Captain Cook arrives in Nootka Sound.
• Mackenzie reaches mouth of Mackenzie River.

1793 Mackenzie reaches Pacific by land.

1805 Simon Fraser establishes NWC fur trade in BC.

1807 Marie Anne Lagimodière first non-native woman in west.

1808 Simon Fraser follows Fraser River to its mouth.

1810 York Factory is headquarters for western fur trade.

Create a chart with the following columns: Dangerous/ Not Dangerous/ Want to Do/ Do Not Want to Do/Have Done. Then look at this collage of activities. List each activity under the appropriate column. Which three of these activities would you most like to do? Least like to do? Why?

had been explored, settled, and lived in for thousands of years by Aboriginal peoples. Most European explorers were guided on their journeys and shown the continent by Aboriginals. These same explorers also quickly became dependent on the First Nations people of North America for basic survival techniques and strategies. Jacques Cartier's expedition might have ended in total failure had Aboriginals not shown him how to make a white cedar tea that quickly healed his desperately ill crew. Time and time again, Aboriginal knowledge and technology allowed the newcomers to survive and thrive in North America. Even the riches of the fur trade were totally dependent on Aboriginal trappers and hunters. They found, caught, killed, and prepared

TIMELINE

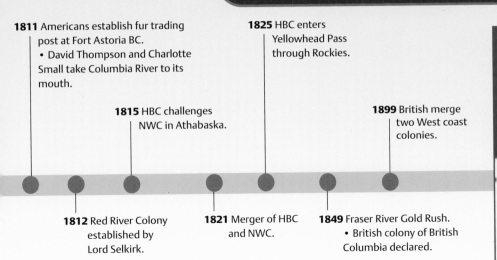

1811 Americans establish fur trading post at Fort Astoria BC.
• David Thompson and Charlotte Small take Columbia River to its mouth.

1825 HBC enters Yellowhead Pass through Rockies.

1815 HBC challenges NWC in Athabaska.

1899 British merge two West coast colonies.

1812 Red River Colony established by Lord Selkirk.

1821 Merger of HBC and NWC.

1849 Fraser River Gold Rush.
• British colony of British Columbia declared.

the valuable beaver pelts, then transported the furs hundreds of miles to the closest trading post. Aboriginal peoples often gave food and shelter to the traders who were far from their settlements. All of the great rivers, lakes, and oceans were well known to the Aboriginal peoples who skillfully taught the newcomers how to survive in their new land.

Heroes and Villains

The life of an explorer was one of great sacrifice and heroic effort. But explorers could also cause problems for those whose land they were exploring. Some explorers were kind, generous, and respectful; others were greedy, jealous, and had little respect for the life and traditions of others. The Age of Exploration not only changed the face of North America, but it also changed forever the lifestyle of those people who had lived there for thousands of years. European explorers brought goods that Aboriginal peoples often found useful. But those same explorers also brought tragedy and death. Many of the Aboriginal peoples died from European diseases they were unable to fight. Trade with Europeans exposed First Nations peoples to deadly weapons and to alcohol, both of which reduced their numbers and weakened their societies and families. Some First Nations went to war against each other for the right to trade with the Europeans. As time went on, many of their traditional skills and activities were lost as Aboriginal peoples worked with, and then for, Europeans. Settlers soon followed the explorers and traders. Trading posts grew into

Telling Their Stories

Hernando Cortez

So, what kind of person would want to be an explorer? Many of the explorers and crew members who came to North America were very young. Some were barely into their teens. Write a paragraph explaining why you think young people were suited for exploration. Then watch the opening vignette of Episode 2 of *Canada: A People's History* (02:00:34 to 02:02:47). What are the risks and rewards of exploration? What characteristics would describe someone who wanted to explore?

villages, towns, and eventually cities. The land that had once been in Aboriginal hands was soon under the control of migrating peoples from across the ocean. In time, the First Nations would lose their freedom to travel, hunt, and live on the land, and be forced to move to areas of land that were "reserved" for them. The European desire for adventure and exploration cost other peoples their culture and lifestyle.

A Multicultural Experience

From earliest times, Canada was a country of many cultures. The Aboriginal peoples who lived here were divided into hundreds of nations with strikingly different languages, traditions, and cultures. Explorers who came from Europe were Portuguese, Spanish, French, English, Dutch, and Russian. Some "national" expeditions were often led by men from other countries. Columbus, an Italian, sailed for Spain. Cabot, also Italian, sailed for England. Some Portuguese worked for the French.

The building of a new North American society, particularly in the Canadian half of the continent, depended on a rich mosaic of peoples. The fur trade was a partnership of English, French, Aboriginals, and a new nation of people called Métis, of mixed Aboriginal-European blood.

The foundations of Canada today rest on the lives and experiences of a tremendous diversity of peoples and cultures. Multiculturalism is not a result of modern immigration practices, but a fact of Canadian identity. Canada has always been multicultural and has progressed because of contributions from all of its people.

Matthew Da Costa

The first Black person in Canada was Matthew Da Costa, a free man of African descent. Skilled in languages, he worked as an interpreter for French explorers in 1608. His knowledge of Mi'kmaq, a First Nations language, was vital to the early exploration of Canada.

◀ Playback ▶

1. **In your opinion, what characteristics does someone need in order to be a successful explorer? Which of these characteristics do you have?**

2. **Explain why explorers did not "discover" anything when they came to North America.**

3. **What was the price of European exploration to Aboriginal peoples?**

CHAPTER I

THREE SEAS

Viking Ship, **H. Oakes–Jones**

Canada is a huge continent surrounded by three great oceans, the Atlantic, the Arctic, and the Pacific. These oceans were both barriers to and highways of exploration.

THE NORSE CROSS THE ATLANTIC

Long before the voyages of Christopher Columbus, North America was visited by the Norse, often called the Vikings. Travelling in their longships around 1000 AD, the Norse explored vast areas of Canada's North. They visited several sites in the Eastern Arctic, including Ellesmere and Baffin Islands.

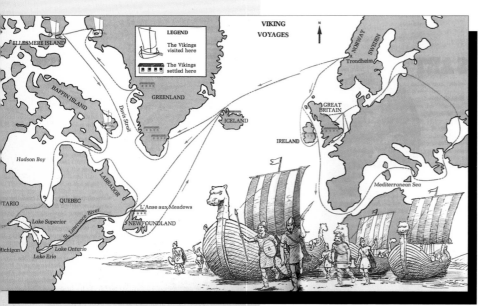

The Norse visited Ellesmere Island and Baffin Island, and even settled for a while at L'Anse-Aux-Meadows.

Around 1000 AD, a small group of Norse explorers, led by Thorfinn Karlsefni, tried to set up a more permanent settlement in North America. This site, known as L'Anse-Aux-Meadows, is the first accepted European settlement in North America and is a United Nations World Heritage Site. Here the Vikings built houses, storage buildings, and an iron smithy.

For some reason though, these early attempts at colonization were abandoned quickly. Maybe the Norse left because of the brutal winters and poor soil. Maybe relations with the Aboriginal peoples turned hostile and violent. (Both Norse and Aboriginal legends describe bloody conflicts in which Aboriginals drove the Norse away.)

Before the Norse left in 1000 AD, however, a baby boy named Snorri Thorbrandsson was born to Karlsefni and his wife, Gudrid. The baby is the first European known to be born on North American soil. When the Vikings sailed away in the northern fog, North America lay "undiscovered" for another half century. It would be nearly 600 years before the more successful settlement led by Samuel de Champlain.

CARTIER CROSSES THE ATLANTIC

In 1534, Francis I of France hired Jacques Cartier, an experienced navigator from St. Malo, France, to "discover certains isles where it is said there must be great quantities of gold and other riches." Although he was interested in exploration, Francis didn't know much about North America. Still, Cartier would be the one

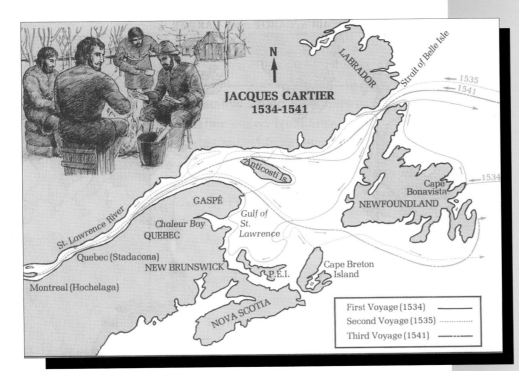

JACQUES CARTIER
1534-1541

First Voyage (1534) ————
Second Voyage (1535) ············
Third Voyage (1541) – – – –

mariner who not only explored the coast of North America but also found a huge river that carved a moving highway deep into the interior of the continent. On the shores of this river, a great French empire would be built, only to transfer to British control at the Battle of Quebec in 1759.

FIRST VOYAGE, 1534

Cartier already knew the way to Newfoundland, having sailed there with fishing fleets in the past. He quickly visited Chaleur Bay and explored the East Coast of North America. He kept excellent notes and made fine maps. He recorded the first trading deal between Europeans and Aboriginals, a spontaneous transaction that would become the foundation of a new economy and the target of jealous and warring empires.

As Cartier prepared to return to home, he erected a cross claiming the land (likely present-day Gaspé, Quebec) for France. Then he did what many European explorers had done: he kidnapped two Iroquois men to show them off in France. Cartier's action was particularly cruel, because the men were the sons of Donnacona, an Iroquois chief whom Cartier had befriended.

In Europe, Taignoagny and Domagaya, the two men, got a lot of attention. Their stories of a rich "Kingdom of the Saguenay" stirred the imagination and greed of the French who quickly decided to send Cartier back to the new lands on the other side of the ocean.

The Man from St. Malo

Cartier made three important voyages to Canada. His exploration of the St. Lawrence River opened the interior of North America to further exploration and settlement. What image of Cartier does the artist present in this painting?

From the Sources

The trade in furs between Aboriginal peoples and Europeans turned out to be a central theme in the history of North America. But this important economic activity started with a simple, spontaneous exchange. Here is how Jacques Cartier recorded the event in his journal.

The next day, some of the Indians came in nine canoes to the point at the mouth of the cove where we lay anchored with our ships. And being informed of their arrival we went with our two long-boats to the point where they were… As soon as they saw us they began to run away, making signs to us that they had come to barter with us; and held up some furs of small value, with which they clothe themselves. We likewise made signs to them that we wished them no harm, and sent two men on shore, to offer them some knives and other iron goods, and a red cap to their chief… The savages showed a marvellously good pleasure in possessing and obtaining these iron wares and other commodities, dancing and going through many ceremonies and throwing salt water over their heads with their hands. They bartered all they had to such an extent that all went back naked without anything on them…

Cartier traded often and fairly with the First Nations. Cartier was not trusted, though, because he was greedy for furs and gold, and unthinkingly kidnapped Aboriginal people. How would you describe the nature of French-Aboriginal relations as shown in the painting? Why?

SECOND VOYAGE, 1535

Cartier returned quickly to North America. Donnacona's sons had now seen the French court, could speak some French, and understood the power of the land from which the traders came. They became Cartier's expert guides and an important link between the European and Aboriginal peoples.

This second voyage was marked by Cartier's discovery of the St. Lawrence River and his voyage deep into the North American interior. He travelled to Hochelaga (present-day Montreal) but couldn't get past the rapids of the St. Lawrence. Turning around, he stayed near the great Aboriginal encampment of Stadacona (present-day Quebec City) where he built a fort and decided to spend the winter.

The winter of 1535 was a long and brutal one that stretched from mid-November to April of the next year. The French were not prepared for the biting winds and freezing cold. Inactivity, sub-zero temperatures, and poor

Without the cedar tea provided by his Aboriginal neighbours, all of Cartier's crew might have died of scurvy. In your view did Cartier treat the Aboriginal peoples fairly? Explain.

nutrition began to reduce their strength. Most of the crew got scurvy, a painful disease caused by a lack of vitamin C. Cartier noted of his crew that:

> *"And all had their mouths so tainted that the gums rotted away down to the roots of the teeth, which nearly fell out. The disease spread among the three ships to such an extent that in the middle of February, of the 110 men forming our company, there were not ten in good health."*

Cartier was still wary of his Aboriginal neighbours. Fifty Aboriginal men died from disease and Cartier thought that they would infect his own men. Hiding the extent of the sickness in his camp from Donnacona's people, Cartier asked them to prepare a medicine (a tea made from white cedar) that he had seen restore the health of the Aboriginals. Those who drank the cedar tea recovered quickly. The treatment was shared with the entire crew who recovered as well. In the spring, as Cartier's crew prepared to leave, Cartier kidnapped 10 Aboriginal men, including Donnacona.

Astrolabe

Compass

The Technology of Exploration

The Age of Exploration was launched with the help of some important technological advances. While primitive by today's standards of satellites and lasers, these tools helped navigators find their way in the far reaches of the New World. The compass helped establish direction. It carried a magnetic lodestone that always pointed north. Users could then determine the other directions. The astrolabe showed distance from the equator. It measured the angle between the sun or the North Star and the horizon. Using these tools together, navigators could pinpoint their position accurately.

Third Voyage, 1541-43

When Cartier returned to France with his captives and his tales of untold riches, he attracted great interest to North America. But European politics was complex and it was several years before another expedition could be mounted. This time, Francis not only wanted riches, he also wanted to convert the Aboriginal peoples to Christianity and to establish a permanent settlement.

Francis put the Sieur de Roberval, a court favourite, in charge of the expedition. Cartier was second in command. Cartier landed first. His crew was a rough and unruly group, many of whom had been plucked from French prisons. After the long and difficult voyage, even they were weakened. Cartier built a fort near Cap Rouge which he called Charlesbourg Royal. He loaded great quantities of what he thought were gold and diamonds into the holds of his vessels.

When Roberval had still not appeared in 1542, Cartier headed back to France. He did cross paths with Roberval in Newfoundland, but refused to stay. Perhaps he was exhausted by the horrible winters. Maybe he was afraid of rising tensions between Europeans and Aboriginal peoples. Without Cartier's experience and support, Roberval was doomed to failure. After a miserable winter in Canada, he too returned to France, in 1543. The French made no further attempts at settlement for many decades.

But Cartier's efforts, and his detailed records of his journeys, were extremely important. Cartier had charted a great North American river, made contact with First Nations, and ignited interest in the mineral wealth of this new land. His efforts helped lay the foundations for the French presence in North America.

◀ Playback ▶

1. **Briefly describe the first European settlement in North America. Why did it fail?**

2. **Why were Cartier's explorations so important?**

3. **What do you like or dislike about Cartier's actions?**

4. **How was the Atlantic Ocean a highway to exploration for Jacques Cartier?**

SEEKING THE NORTHWEST PASSAGE

For many centuries, most nations saw Canada as an obstacle in the way of the fabled riches of the Far East. Most of the people who explored Canada were simply trying to go around or through it in order to reach Asia. They knew little about Canada's fabulous and abundant wealth. For over 300 years, Europeans struggled to find a way to the East through the Northwest Passage, a rumoured easy route across the top of North America, via the Arctic Ocean. The rugged, dangerous Canadian Arctic, however, would swallow up dozens of ships and lead hundreds to frozen deaths.

Arctic exploration is a powerful story of bravery, greed, violence, deceit, and tragedy, all elements of the stories of Martin Frobisher and Henry Hudson. There really is no easy route over Canada's northern waters. Even today, though some have crossed the Arctic, it is not an important sea lane to Asia.

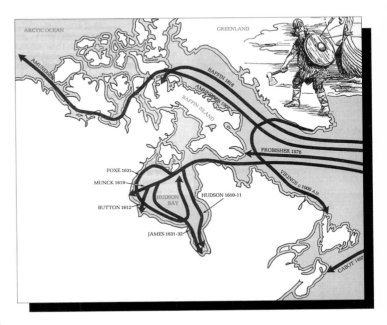

MARTIN FROBISHER, SEA DOG (1539-94)

The first Englishman into the Arctic, Frobisher was a tough sailor and a skilled navigator. He had served aboard slave ships and pirate ships. He had once bragged that finding a route to the East would be "easie to be performed." He couldn't have been more wrong. Despite making three voyages to the Arctic from 1567-1578, Frobisher never found the passage. He was given the lordly title of High Admiral of Cathay (Cathay was the ancient term for China), but was never even remotely close to the shores of that nation.

Frobisher's meetings with the Inuit of the Arctic usually ended up in confrontations. He once captured four Inuit to take home to England, as proof that he was in the northern reaches of Asia. He was completely fooled by their features. Tragically, his prisoners, including a young child, died quickly.

Martin Frobisher

Many Arctic explorers were disrespectful to the people who already lived in the region. The groups had a mutual fear and suspicion, and they often clashed violently. This painting of a battle between the Inuit and English was created by a member of Frobisher's crew. Frobisher didn't help the situation when he kidnapped four Inuit to take them to England. In a struggle in the Arctic, which group do you think had the advantage? Why?

Although Frobisher did not find the passage to China, he did bring back to England hundreds of tonnes of what he thought was gold. But it was iron pyrite, "fool's gold," and worthless.

His expeditions failed, but Frobisher did map and explore the Arctic waters. In his later career, he earned glory fighting the Spanish and died in the service of England.

THE TRAGEDY OF HENRY HUDSON
(Dates unknown, late 1500s to approx. 1611)

Another skilled navigator and sailor was Henry Hudson, whose dreams of finding a passage across North America ended in tragedy. Hudson had already tried to sail across the continent twice. His final expedition to find the Northwest Passage began April 7, 1760. Sailing for English merchants, he left England for North America on the ship, *Discovery*. By his own calculations, he was confident he would reach the Far East by February.

Hudson, however, was not a good leader. He changed his mind a lot and played favourites, and had faced mutiny on earlier voyages. Many crew members on this voyage were unruly and untrustworthy. But Hudson was so confident that this great adventure would end in success that he brought along his teenage son, Jack. On this voyage, Hudson bravely faced every challenge the sea and ice hurled forth, including crossing the "furious

Henry Hudson

overfall," a spectacular barrier of ice, fog, wind, and sub-zero temperatures which we now know as the Hudson Strait.

Having entered the bay, Hudson was sure that the way to the East was now clear. But after sailing around the bay and finding no exit, Hudson and his crew became frozen in the ice and were stranded for a long, miserable winter. The men fought, argued and plotted against each other. When it was safe to sail again, Hudson prepared to continue to the East. His crew was furious — the men wanted to return home, and many of them mutinied. They put Hudson, his son, and a few ill sailors on a small boat and set them adrift. Those on the small boat were never seen or heard from again.

Most of the mutineers died on the way home. The survivors barely made it, living on candlewax and seaweed. One survivor, Rober Bylot, became an Arctic explorer himself.

Aboriginal peoples of the area tell stories about white sailors who were abandoned, then killed. One young boy was spared, and was adopted into the tribe. What really happened in the bay that now bears Hudson's name? Nobody knows: the Arctic holds many secrets about the explorers who did not respect its power.

In 1970, the ship *Hudson 70* completed a Northwest Passage across the top of North America. The RCMP vessel *St. Roch* completed the first west-east passage in 1942.

Yes, Hudson was a difficult leader. But was it right to abandon him, his son, and his sick crew? That seems like a very cruel thing to do. The mutineers who survived were never tried or convicted. What other options do you think the mutineers might have had?

◄ Playback ►

1. **What did the English Arctic explorers hope to find? How successful were they?**

2. **What do you think of the career of Martin Frobisher?**

3. **Explain whether you think Hudson deserved his fate.**

4. **Was the Arctic Ocean a barrier or a highway to exploration? Explain.**

THE PACIFIC COAST

Explorers were interested in the western coast of North America too, but full-scale settlement there was harder. There was no river like the St. Lawrence to help explorers get deep into the interior, and huge mountain ranges made exploration difficult. There are tales of legendary explorations made by Chinese and Japanese sailors although there is little convincing proof. Spanish, Russian, English, and American sailors all actively explored the Northwest coast during the 18th century. For some, it was a continuation of the lure of the Northwest Passage. Perhaps a western outlet could be found, since the eastern entrance seemed so difficult to find.

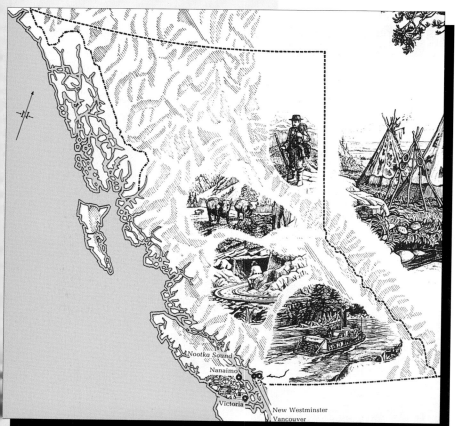

CAPTAIN COOK

One of the most well-known navigators of the late 18th century was Captain James Cook. A world adventurer and skilled cartographer, Cook had explored and surveyed the coasts of New Zealand, Australia, Newfoundland, Labrador, and the St. Lawrence channel. He skillfully charted the waters around Louisbourg and the St. Lawrence, giving General Wolfe the important information he needed to defeat the French at both Louisbourg and Quebec. He had already completed a circumnavigation of the world when in 1776 the British Royal Navy assigned him to chart the Northwest coast of North America. In his search for the Northwest Passage, Cook landed at Nootka Sound to repair his ships and trade with the local Aboriginal peoples. He later found out that the sea otter pelts he received were of stunning value in Asia, and the Northwest sea otter trade was born. Soon the ships of many nations were sailing to this once isolated coast in search of the lucrative furs. Unfortunately, Captain Cook's brilliant career was cut short in a battle on the Hawaiian Islands.

Captain James Cook

Village at Nootka Sound.

THE FIRST CHINESE SETTLEMENT

The first Chinese people to settle in North America came in 1789. About 50 Chinese men were part of the crew on the boat of John Meares, a former British naval officer. Meares was eager to earn his fortune in the sea otter trade. He and his crew built a small post on Vancouver Island. Meares hoped to establish a chain of forts along the Northwest coast to seize control of the otter fur trade. He and his workers also built the first ship manufactured on the Pacific coast of North America, the *North West America*. But Spanish forces seized the ship and closed down the settlement. Some of the Chinese workers returned home, but others melted into the forest and joined existing Aboriginal communities. Later visitors to the region noted that some Nootka people appeared to have Chinese features and practised Asian customs. Over time, this small Chinese community became integrated into Nootka culture.

Some of the earliest Chinese settlers on Canada's west coast eventually became part of the Nootka nation.

Telling Their Stories

JOHN JEWITT

John Jewitt was a 19-year-old blacksmith on board the American ship *Boston*. When the ship sailed into Nootka harbour to trade for furs in 1803, Jewitt's life was changed forever.

Relations between Aboriginal peoples and Europeans were often friendly. Both sides were curious about the other. Both gained wealth and power from the fur trade. But some Europeans, like the captain of the Boston, were disrespectful of Aboriginal peoples. The captain met with Maquinna, the Nootka chief and an important leader to the other coastal First Nations. The captain gave Maquinna a gun, but Maquinna broke it, and the captain humiliated the chief by scolding him in front of his warriors.

Maquinna and his warriors took their revenge. They massacred the entire crew of the *Boston* and destroyed the ship. But they spared the life of Jewitt. As he explains in his journal, his skills saved his life:

"He then asked me if I would be his slave during my life—if I would fight for him in his battles, if I would repair his muskets and make daggers and knives for him..."

Afraid, Jewitt quickly accepted. Jewitt travelled with Maquinna, who soon came to see him as a son. He married a Nootka woman and met other great nations such as the Salish, Haida, Kwakiutl, and Makah. He came to admire and respect his captors, eventually becoming a reluctant friend.

But Jewitt was still a captive, and he wanted to return to his own society. In 1805, he eventually escaped. He settled in Connecticut, where he wrote a play, a book, and a song detailing his life in captivity.

View the clip *Captivity* (02:51:16 to 02:57:27) from Episode 1 of *Canada: A People's History*. From his journals, we know a lot about Jewitt. What does Jewitt say about the way that some traders treated Aboriginal peoples? Why do you think Jewitt chose to escape? Describe his escape plan and explain what it shows about Jewitt as a person.

In spite of their great differences, the Aboriginal chief, Maquinna, and John Jewitt, a captive US blacksmith, developed a friendship and mutual respect.

From the Sources

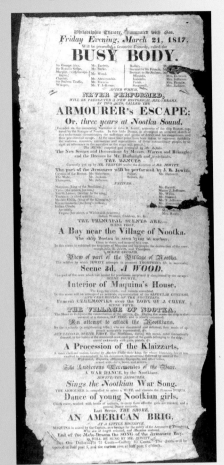

Part of the playbill advertising Jewitt's play about his experiences at Nootka Sound

◄ Playback ►

1. What groups of people showed interest in the Pacific coast of North America?

2. The Pacific Ocean is one barrier to exploring Canada from the west. How did Cook turn this barrier into a highway?

3. What is the importance of the Meares settlement on Vancouver Island?

4. Either as Maquinna or John Jewitt, write a brief farewell note to the other.

History in Action First Encounters

The Back Story

The first encounters between Europeans and Aboriginal peoples in North America must have been remarkable events. Neither group would have encountered people like the other. Communication between the two groups, considering their different culture and language, would have been difficult. Yet both groups showed courage and curiosity, and eagerly pursued further contact. Europeans left a few records of these encounters. But the First Nations peoples had no written language, so no definitive accounts of their first impressions exist.

The Goal

In role as an Aboriginal person at the time of the first European explorers, create an illustrated account of the first meeting between North American Aboriginals and Europeans.

The Steps

1. Choose one of the encounters presented in this chapter.
2. Review the material about the encounter, then review other resources such as books, the Internet, and Episode 1, Hour 2, of *Canada: A People's History*.
3. Imagine that you are an Aboriginal Canadian encountering a European for the first time. What might you think about these strange people? Make notes about how you might view them physically (their clothing, ships, tools, language, gestures, and so on) and emotionally (do they seem friendly, threatening, skilled, weak?)
4. From the Aboriginal point of view, write and illustrate a one- to two-page account of the first meeting you have chosen. Include some captions to describe the meeting further.

Evaluating Your Work

These are the criteria you should think about as you complete your work. Your work should:
- Show your chosen story in a clear sequence of illustrations
- Describe your chosen story in text that supports and expands on the illustrations
- Be based on historical fact and context
- Be of the correct length
- Be clearly and neatly drawn and written, with no errors in spelling or grammar

The earliest illustrations of Aboriginal peoples may not be accurate or authentic. European artists may have focused too much on one feature because they were ne always skilled observers, they often drew from memory, an they were unfamiliar with the look of these people they were seeing for the first time An Aboriginal artist might face the same limitations when drawing a European.

CHAPTER 2

THE FUR TRADE OPENS THE CONTINENT

Castor du Canada

For much of our history, the beaver remained a symbol of Canada's wealth. What do you think would best represent the wealth of Canada today? Explain your choice.

Adventure was not the only thing that explorers were seeking in North America. If they wanted to keep returning, they needed an economic reason. Fur became that reason. The fur trade was started by accident. When the first fishing crews visited Canada's Atlantic shores, the fishers spent some time on land drying their catch and mending their nets. The first Aboriginal people that they met seemed willing to trade goods. The two civilizations were wary of each other but often friendly and curious. Very quickly the Europeans exchanged pots and tools for the furs that the Aboriginal peoples carried on their backs. Although it started as a sideline, the fur trade soon became the key economic component of Canadian settlement and exploration.

The entire economy of Canada once depended on a small, furry animal that cuts down trees with its teeth and builds dams out of sticks. On the strength of the partnership between Indian trappers and European traders, a country took shape.

Daniel Francis in *Horizon Canada,* **Volume 4 p. 73**

BEAVER HUNTING in CANADA.

THE BEAVER

Europeans first wanted beaver fur pelts out of curiosity. Later, they used the pelts to make coats. But the pelts weren't particularly valuable. About 1580, however, things changed. In men's fashion, broad-brimmed felt hats became the rage in Europe, especially among the rich. What was the best material for making the felt? Beaver fur. Very few beaver were left in Europe, but they were plentiful in North America.

All beaver fur makes good felt, but some furs are more valuable than others. Most of the furs that traders first brought to Europe had already been worn by the Aboriginal peoples who traded them. These furs were *castor gras* or greasy fur — the outer guard hairs had worn away and only the very soft fur was left. These furs were highly prized and very valuable. When the demand for beaver fur became greater than the supply, traders began shipping untreated furs, *castor sec*, which were much less valuable.

The fur trade was risky and even dangerous, but for 200 years it brought great riches to those who succeeded. The industry slowed down when the supply of furs dwindled and fashions changed. People still trap beaver today, but the fur is used mainly for coats, not hats.

RADISSON AND DES GROSEILLIERS: CAESARS IN THE WILDERNESS

Pierre Radisson and Médard Chouart des Groseilliers were two adventurers who would stop at nothing to succeed in riches and glory in North America. While seeking furs, trade routes, and adventure, they moved deep into the continent and set in motion a brutal war for its control. They risked their lives, they became amazingly rich, they lost huge fortunes, they fought and worked for two countries. Theirs is one of the great stories of Canadian history.

SUCCESS AT ANY COST

Pierre Esprit Radisson came to New France in 1651 when he was only 15 years old. Within a year, he had been captured by Mohawks and adopted by a Mohawk family, going on hunts and war parties. Brave and cunning, he escaped from captivity and torture twice more. When he returned to New France, he joined his brother-in-law, Médard Chouart, Sieur des Groseilliers (born in 1618), in working with the Jesuits at their mission at Saine-Marie-Among-the-Huron.

In 1654-1656, des Groseilliers had led a successful fur trading expedition to Lake Michigan. He returned safely with 50 canoes heavy with rich pelts. He had made a fortune.

Keen to earn even greater wealth, Radisson and des Groseilliers proposed another mission to the shores of Lake Superior. The governor did not trust them. He insisted that two of his own men go along. Radisson and des Groseilliers didn't want the inexperienced men on the mission, so they slipped off in the middle of the night. Although he didn't like rules, Radisson was a valuable partner: he had a lot of knowledge about Aboriginal languages and culture and knew the geography of the interior well. After a long winter and a successful spring trade with many Native traders, the two men returned to New France with a rich load of furs.

WILL THE DREAM DIE?

Radisson and des Groseilliers now knew that furs were plentiful in the rivers to the north. They had also heard that those rivers might lead to a great salt-water bay — and a new supply route. They had a dream of sending ships into the bay to trade with the Aboriginals, then sending the furs directly to France. This new northern route would be a fast and inexpensive way to get to the furs. It was more direct than the route through the Great Lakes and along the St. Lawrence River. It would also help the traders avoid the Iroquois, with whom the French were at war. The two men were eager to present their riches to the French governor and start making their dream a reality.

Telling Their Stories

The voyageurs were the brute strength of the fur trade. They paddled and carried huge canoes filled with trade goods, supplies, and traders from Montreal to Hudson Bay. View the clip *The Voyageurs* (36:04-40:31), Episode 6 of *Canada: A People's History*. What do you think life must have been like for the voyageurs? Imagine you are Joseph Grenier's son. Respond to your father's letter, describing what your life has been like for the past five years.

Shooting the Rapids (Quebec),
Frances Ann Hopkins

But the governor was angry at the men for disobeying his orders. He fined them, took away their furs, and jailed des Groseilliers. Their dreams were collapsing. The two adventurers decided to sell their idea to the English.

The English sent two ships, the *Eaglet* and the *Nonsuch* into the Bay for furs in 1668. Only the *Nonsuch* reached Hudson Bay but it returned in 1669 with a wealth of furs obtained from Aboriginal peoples who had traded with the Europeans. The scheme had worked. Quickly, the English created a new company, Hudson's Bay Company (HBC), to trade for furs in the region. Heavily supported by the King's cousin, Prince Rupert, HBC would soon establish a string of forts at the mouths of the rivers that emptied into Hudson Bay. From there the furs were transported directly to England. Radisson and des Groseilliers had helped launch a great company and opened up the vast

The first English ship into the bay in 1668 was the *Nonsuch*. Its successful trading season led to the creation of HBC. To celebrate the 300th anniversary of HBC, an exact replica of the *Nonsuch* was built and sailed along Canadian waterways. Today it is in the Manitoba Museum in Winnipeg.

interior of North America to further trade and exploration. The rich furs of the North and West were headed for England, not France.

Later Radisson would be lured back to work for a new French company on the Bay, the Compagnie du Nord. When that failed, he once again found himself in the employ of HBC, so valued were his skills and experience. He later retired to London and wrote of his adventures.

Hudson's Bay Company

One lasting result of Radisson's and des Groseiller's exploits was the creation of Hudson's Bay Company. Formed in 1670, it is one of the oldest companies in the world. Originally headquartered in London, England, the company moved to Winnipeg in 1970. Its department store division is still known as "the Bay."

THE BATTLE FOR THE BAY

When the French realized that HBC was draining furs to the North, they decided to protect their interests. They sent Father Albanel, a Jesuit missionary and explorer, to the Bay in 1671 to check on English activities. He found a thriving English–Aboriginal fur trading exchange. The French were not going to give up without a fight. They sent raiding parties to harass and capture the English forts on the bay. One of New France's greatest warriors was Pierre Le Moyne d'Iberville, known to the English as the "scourge of the bay." He attacked many of the forts by land and drove out the English. He was a skilled sailor and, in one of the greatest battles along the icy frontier, led one ship, the *Pelican*, against three English warships. When the smoke of battle had cleared, one English ship lay at the bottom of the sea and another had been driven aground. The third ship surrendered. D'Iberville was master of the bay. By 1700, the English had lost all but one post.

The French, however, faced losses in other areas of the world. They eventually had to give up control of Hudson Bay, signing it over to the British in the 1713 Treaty of Utrecht.

King Charles II grants the royal charter to create the HBC in 1670.

Pierre Le Moyne d'Iberville

Born in New France, d'Iberville was perhaps New France's most famous warrior. He fought for French interests all over North America. He drove the English from Hudson Bay for a time.

D'Iberville fought fiercely for New France on land and sea. In his ship the *Pelican*, he defeated three English ships carrying over 114 cannons. Identify d'Iberville's ship in this painting.

◀Playback▶

1. Describe the origins of the fur trade.

2. In your view, were Radisson and des Groseilliers traitors?

3. Briefly describe the exploits of d'Iberville.

4. Do you think the fur trade was worth fighting over? What things send nations to war today?

5. What goods or products have you traded or do you trade? Why?

Fur fairs were an important part of the fur trade.

Away from the Bay: The French Adventure in North America

Although driven from Hudson Bay by the Treaty of Utrecht, French explorers and traders did not lose total control of the fur trade. The traders of HBC were happy to stay in their little posts along the shores of Hudson Bay, but the French were prepared to drive deep into the interior of North America. Instead of waiting for Aboriginal traders to bring the furs to them, the French chose to go to the Aboriginals and intercept the furs for New France. In this struggle to gain control over the fur trade, much of North America was first explored. In some ways, Canada was a product of the competition between French and English traders. While most of the East and North had been explored, the South and West hadn't been claimed yet.

THE DRIVE TO THE WEST

The French were prepared to outwork the English. They would travel further and deeper into the North American wilderness to meet Aboriginal trappers long before they reached the HBC posts. This shortened the trip for the trappers but meant long months deep in the dangerous wilderness and much back-breaking work to return the furs thousands of kilometres to Montreal. It was a high price, but the French were willing to pay it.

A FAMILY AFFAIR

Much of the exploration of the Northwest was the work of one remarkable family, the La Vérendryes. From 1731-1743, Pierre de La Vérendrye and his nephew and four sons pushed back the frontiers of New France to the foothills of the Rockies. They heard of a great western sea and dared to think they might reach it. They built a chain of forts west of Lake Superior that re-established the French fur trade. The courage and daring of these six men built a French North American empire that stretched from the Atlantic coast to the Rocky Mountains. It was a brilliant achievement, but it cost one of Pierre's sons his life. At the end of his travels, Pierre de La Vérendrye was worn, saddened, and in financial trouble. He wrote:

Pierre de La Vérendrye

> *People do not know me: money has never been my object; I have sacrificed myself and my sons for the service of His Majesty and the good of the colony; what advantages shall result from my toils only the future may tell.*

In the short term, the advantages were clearly for New France. In the long term, his work opened much of North America to future generations. His tiny posts later became the sites of such great cities as Winnipeg and Calgary.

The explorations of La Vérendrye

Louis Jolliet and Père
Marquette paddled along
the Mississippi River
and into Spanish territory.
Research to find out
why Spain wanted land
in North America. Why
would French explorers
turn around when they
discovered they were
on Spain's land?

TO THE MISSISSIPPI

Louis Jolliet was a fur trader and explorer. Père Marquette was
a Jesuit missionary. Both had considerable experience in the
wilderness. In 1673 they were commissioned to search for the
famous Mississippi River. With only five voyageurs in their crew,
they paddled and portaged from Green Bay, Wisconsin, to the
upper reaches of the Mississippi. They paddled nearly 1000 km
along its length before realizing that they were headed for the
Gulf of Mexico and into Spanish territory. They returned to
New France without completing their mission. Yet they had
found another rich fur-trading area whose rivers made the transport of pelts easier than that of the Great Lakes–Hudson Bay
route. Their report noted the vast areas of rich, flat land for
farming, the many minerals and the new fruits that they discovered. For the people living along the often freezing and inhos-
pitable St. Lawrence, the lure of the Mississippi was strong.

MUTINY ON THE MISSISSIPPI

Jolliet and Marquette were unsuccessful. It was left to a very
difficult, troubled man to complete the voyage down the
Mississippi River. René Robert Cavalier de La Salle was a
successful fur trader but a difficult person to get along with.
Some believe he was mentally unstable. In 1679, he built and
launched the *Griffon*, the first ship to sail the Great Lakes.
In 1682, he led an expedition to the mouth of the Mississippi

and claimed the land — Louisiana — for King Louis XIV of
France. La Salle's long trip opened up more land to New France
than had any voyage since those of Cartier.

Though one of the greatest explorers of his time, La Salle
was not particularly liked by his men. After attempting to return
to France via the sea, La Salle and his crew found themselves
many kilometres west, in Texas. A more likable man might have
been able to control his crew in such a trying situation. This was
not the case for La Salle. His crew mutineed and shot him.

THEY SLEPT BY THE BAY

Although the HBC soon learned of the French drive into the
interior, they still preferred to stay by the bay and await the
arrival of pelts. Explorers Henry Kelsey and Anthony Henday
travelled further into the Northwest in search of furs but their
efforts were not followed up by the company. It wasn't until
much later that HBC's leaders decided to explore the interior as
aggressively as the French had.

La Salle expanded the
French empire in North
America in a dramatic way,
but he was a poor leader.
List the qualities you think a
good leader should have.
Why are those qualities
important for leading a suc-
cessful exploration mission?
View the clip *To the Upper
Country* (10:04:13 to
10:12:04), Episode 3 of
Canada: A People's History.
Which qualities of leader-
ship did La Salle have?
Which did he not have?

THE FUR TRADE AND NEW FRANCE

The fur trade helped expand New France from the shores of the Atlantic, west to the foothills of the Rockies, and south to the mouth of the mighty Mississippi River. But

Traders leave Montreal to go west.

New France was a shallow colony. There were few settlers and few thriving communities. The French spent a lot of their time competing with the English and battling Aboriginals for control of the fur trade. Most of the young, energetic men of the colony preferred the adventure and reward of the fur trade to the less exciting but demanding work of farming, and the French couldn't defend their colony from attacks by the English. In 1759, at the Plains of Abraham, France lost control of New France to English forces. The Treaty of Paris, signed in 1763, gave full control of New France to the English. The "French Adventure" in North America was over. From now on, the fur trade and exploration would be controlled by the English.

THE FUR TRADE AND ABORIGINAL PEOPLES

At first, many Aboriginal peoples were pleased with the new products they got from the Europeans in exchange for their old clothes. Soon, though, they found that they were losing their land, their traditions, and their lives as a result of the fur trade. Diseases swept through Aboriginal villages killing the majority of the residents. Warfare among Aboriginal nations became more deadly with the use of European weaponry. The search for furs undermined the traditional lifestyle and values of the Aboriginal peoples. Receiving alcohol for furs had a disastrous effect on the social framework of Aboriginal society. In the end, weakened by disease, war, and alcohol, many First Nations became dependent on the Europeans and endured the

humiliation of losing their lifestyle and traditional lands. Aboriginal peoples started out as partners in the fur trade, but they ended up as pawns. Life for Canada's First Nations has never been the same.

The First Nations trappers traded their furs for many things from the Europeans, including alcohol. Why do you think many officials told traders they were forbidden to trade it?

◀ Playback ▶

1. **How did the French respond to the English control of the fur trade at Hudson Bay?**

2. **Compare the careers of La Vérendrye and La Salle. In your view who was the greater explorer? Why?**

3. **How did the fur trade hinder the growth of New France?**

4. **Was the fur trade good or bad for the Aboriginal peoples? Explain.**

History in Action   First Encounters

The Back Story
There were many dramatic encounters and events as fur traders explored and opened up the continent of North America.

The Goal
Choose one of the dramatic events described in this chapter, then write a script for, and perform, a three- to five-minute play about the event. You may present your performance on video tape.

Shooting the Rapids (Quebec),
Frances Ann Hopkins

The Steps
1. Form a small group with no more than five members.
2. Choose one historical event from this chapter to dramatize. Consider:
   • Radisson and des Groseilliers "pitching" their idea to English merchants
   • D'Iberville planning an attack on HBC forts
   • La Salle reaching the mouth of the Mississipi River
3. Research the event further using print and electronic sources.
4. Create and write your script and assign roles. Although the story must be based on true events, the dialogue will be creative and original.
5. Consider costumes, staging, and lighting. Low lighting and simple costumes can be very effective.
6. As a group, revise the script until you are satisfied. Rehearse several times so that all participants can perform without notes.
7. Present your play to the class. Be prepared to answer follow-up questions.

Evaluating Your Work
These are the criteria you should think about as you complete your work. Your work should:
   • Be based on historical events
   • Be clearly written and committed to memory
   • Be carefully rehearsed and clearly presented
   • Be presented with careful attention to costuming, staging, and lighting
   • Be of the required length

CHAPTER 3

BATTLE FOR THE WEST

Brigade of Boats, Paul Kane

Explorer and painter Paul Kane travelled the western fur routes from 1846 to 1848. He sketched traders, voyageurs, and Aboriginal people in their natural surroundings. The paintings he made from those sketches have given us a lasting record of the western fur trade.

After the British conquest, French Canada played less of a leadership role in the fur trade. Many merchants returned to France. They were replaced by English-speaking merchants and traders from the Thirteen Colonies and Britain, particularly those from Scotland. Although the HBC traders at first appeared to be dominant, they were soon challenged by new traders working out of Montreal. A group of these traders formed a powerful new company called the North West Company. Competition in the fur trade soon heated up, leading to violence and war. It also led to the rapid exploration of much of the Canadian Northwest.

35

THE CHALLENGERS IN THE FUR WARS

Look at the company flags on the chart below. Write a description of each one. Why do you think each flag is an appropriate symbol of its company? Which flag do you prefer? Why?

Hudson's Bay Company and the North West Company were in the same business but they had different approaches. Review the brief profiles below and decide what you feel are the major similarities and differences between these two great enterprises.

FEATURE	HBC (HUDSON'S BAY COMPANY)	NWC (NORTH WEST COMPANY)
DATE FOUNDED	1670	1784
WHERE FOUNDED	London, England	Montreal, Canada
DATE CLOSED	Still in operation	Merged with HBC in 1821
GEOGRAPHIC CONCENTRATION	Posts at mouths of rivers entering Hudson Bay	The Canadian Northwest, including the Athabaska region
MAJOR POSTS	York Factory, Red River	Fort William, Fort Chipewyan
NUMBER OF POSTS BY 1821	76	97
MAJOR EXPLORERS	Henry Kelsey, Anthony Henday, Samuel Hearne, John Rae	Peter Pond, Alexander Mackenzie, Simon Fraser, David Thompson
STRENGTHS	• Solid economic base • Many years of experience • Lower prices for goods • Furs brought to them	• Went into the wilderness to get the furs • Aggressive, experienced traders • Explored widely • Close ties to Aboriginal peoples
WEAKNESSES	• Lack of adventure • Far from newer fur sources	• Long routes to transfer furs • Internal arguing • Could be aggressive and violent • Less stable financially than HBC

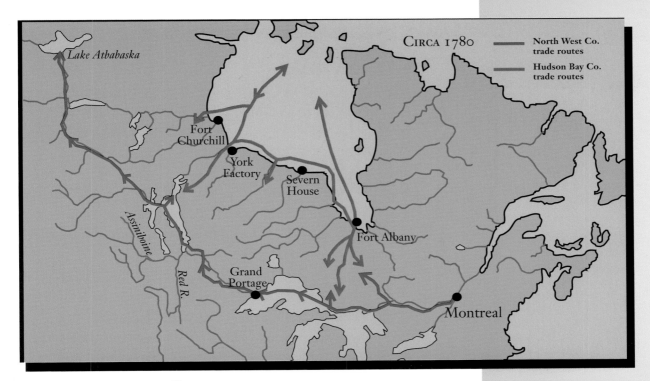

THE SELKIRK SETTLEMENT

The competition between HBC and the NWC became more serious when HBC tried to build a permanent settlement on the land at the forks of the Assiniboine River and the Red River. The land belonged to HBC but was an important part of the NWC route to the west. The Métis of the area, the offspring of European traders and Aboriginal peoples, were not happy with the settlement, either.

The settlement was the idea of Lord Selkirk, a Scottish man who had purchased control of HBC. He had already established colonies of Scots in PEI and in Upper Canada. Although he wanted to help the poor of his country, he also knew that successful settlements would be a stable source of workers for HBC.

The Nor'Westers (as the NWC men were called) were prepared to fight settlement. As one put it, "[Selkirk] must be driven to abandon it for his success would strike at the very existence of our trade." For the NWC, the area was a vital source of food and a main transportation corridor for bringing furs from the Northwest to Fort William, the major supply and exchange fort. Further, the NWC rejected HBC ownership of the territory. The two companies had already been involved in a bruising, brutal battle for control of the fur trade. The Selkirk settlement was yet another source of conflict.

For 10 shillings Lord Selkirk purchased nearly 400 square kilometres of land, five times larger than his native Scotland. He had gained control of HBC and hoped to build a colony at the forks of the Assinboine and Red Rivers to settle impoverished Scottish farmers. The NWC thought Selkirk's proposed settlement would interfere with its trading abilities. Do you agree or disagree? Do you think Selkirk chose this location to disrupt the NWC? Explain.

Money, Money, Money

The piece below is a form of money designed by HBC to show the value of items available for trade. Each coin stood for one prime beaver skin in good condition. The prices of various items were stated in "made beaver" (MB). On which Canadian coin is the beaver shown today?

Just like rival stores today, HBC and the NWC tried to please their customers with the range and quality of what they traded. Aboriginal trappers wanted silver goods and the NWC was happy to provide them. To keep up, HBC had to trade these valued goods, too.

THE SETTLERS

The first settlers to the west endured a long and difficult voyage from Scotland to York Factory on Hudson Bay. They arrived in 1812. The first winters were miserable. The settlers might not have survived without the aid of the Salteaux leader, Peguis, who unselfishly declared:

These are not my lands, they belong to our great Father, for it is only He who gives us the means of existence; for what would become of us if He left us to ourselves? We would wither like the grass on the plains.

The Nor'Westers and the Métis were not so understanding. Each year more and more settlers arrived and more land was cultivated. The Nor'Westers and the Métis saw the cluster of homes and barns as a threat to their livelihood and land. In 1814, the governor of the settlement

The trading post at Fort William was a central part of the long NWC network. Every year, there was a great Rendez-Vous when the *canots de nord,* heavy with furs, reached the post to greet the larger canoes carrying supplies, provisions and trade goods for the coming season. Merchants, clerks, traders, *voyageurs* and Aboriginal peoples spent much time and energy trading, socializing, and exchanging news before they returned home. The trading post was celebrated with this special stamp from Canada Post.

banned food exports from the colony. The Métis provided pemmican that the Nor'Westers depended on. The ban on exports would be a disaster for both groups. Tempers flared.

"You must assist me in driving away the colony. If they are not drove away, the consequence will be that they will prevent you from hunting. They will starve your families, and they will put their feet in the neck of those that attempt to resist them. You can easily see how they mean to finish by what they have begun already."

Duncan Cameron, NWC

The two groups began to terrorize the isolated settlers, trampling fields, firing weapons in the night and burning property.

They immediately began to burn our houses in the day time, and fire upon us during the night, saying the country was theirs, if we did not immediately quit the settlement, they would plunder us of our property, and burn the houses over our heads.

John Pritchard, settler

The NWC arrested the governor and sent the settlers packing. But the settlers returned, with HBC help. In 1816, open war broke out on the plains as the two companies seized each other's forts. When the governor of the Selkirk settlement tried to stop a band of Métis led by Cuthbert Grant near a spot known as The Seven Oaks, shots were fired. Within 15 minutes, 20 settlers and their governor lay dead. The Métis lost one man. The settlers were no match for the Métis marksmen.

Lord Selkirk returned to the settlement, bringing new settlers and a band of retired Swiss soldiers. He seized the great NWC post at Fort William in 1817. Fortunately, cooler heads prevailed and, under pressure from the British government, the two bitter rivals were merged in 1821 under the banner of HBC. The fur wars were over. The tiny settlement was reborn and within 50 years would enter confederation as the province of Manitoba. Furs represented the history of the West but farming was to be its future.

This is a painting of Peguis, chief of the Saulteaux. What impression of him do you get from the painting? Whose perspective do you think is being shared? Peguis was a steady friend of the settlement at Red River. Later, he would regret his easy friendship when he saw his lands overwhelmed by waves of new settlers.

Métis leader Cuthbert Grant (top), and Lord Selkirk, sponsor of the Red River Settlement (bottom), had different views of the future of the West. These different visions erupted into violence. Do you think bloodshed might have been avoided? How?

FIRST EUROPEAN WOMAN IN THE WEST: MARIE ANNE LAGIMODIÈRE

No European women joined the traders and *voyageurs* who scoured the west for furs. The men often found wives

and companions among the Aboriginal peoples. The first European woman to settle permanently in the West was Marie Anne Lagimodière. Born Marie Anne Gaboury, at Maskinonge, Quebec in 1780, she married Jean-Baptiste Lagimodière, a voyageur, in 1806. She accompanied her new husband on the dangerous and demanding 3200 km trip from Montreal to the west. In 1807, she gave birth to Reine, her first daughter and the first European child born in the west. Later she and her husband moved to Red River to await the arrival of the Selkirk settlers. Her husband was sent to warn Lord Selkirk of the problems at Red River but was captured by the NWC for a time. Marie and her husband raised eight children, one of whom was the mother of Louis Riel. Marie died in 1875, at the age of 95.

◄ Playback ►

1. **Would you have preferred to work for Hudson's Bay Company or for the North West Company? Why?**

2. **What events led to the massacre at Seven Oaks?**

3. **How might the massacre have been avoided?**

4. **What was the final result of the conflict between HBC and the NWC?**

Trapper, **Leloir**

THE CHANGING LIVES OF THE FIRST NATIONS

One of the results of the increased contact between Aboriginal peoples and European traders was the spread of deadly epidemics. It is estimated that some First Nations in eastern Canada declined by 78-98 percent of their population by 1600. As the fur trade expanded deep into the North and West of Canada, horrific diseases from Europe continued to wipe out entire Aboriginal communities. These epidemics included typhus, scarlet fever, whooping cough, measles, influenza and perhaps the most deadly — smallpox.

Pierre La Vérendrye noted the first recorded epidemic in 1736-37. He claimed it was a result of the English traders at Hudson Bay. Another epidemic, which broke out in 1781-82, may have resulted in the deaths of 50 percent of the Plains Indians. Yet another outbreak killed about 50-75 percent of the affected tribes in 1837-38. A final, major epidemic occurred in 1869-70.

"We shall never again be the same people."
Saukamappee, a Cree

The results of this deadly assault were many:

- The Aboriginal population of Canada may have collapsed from about 1 000 000 in 1500 to about 125 000 in 1867.
- Entire nations died out.
- Many Aboriginal peoples were too weak to resist any further the arrival of European traders and settlers.
- Many Aboriginal peoples became dependent on Europeans for their survival.
- Some people turned away from the traditional beliefs and from their leaders which together had not saved them.

"When at length it left us and we moved about to find our people, it was no longer with the song and the dance, but with tears, shrieks and howlings of despair for those who would never return to us... We believed the Good Spirit had forsaken us, and allowed the Bad Spirit to become our master."

Saukamapee

Smallpox and other diseases helped destroy the culture and structure of Aboriginal society. It would be the last half of the 20th century before Canada's Aboriginal peoples could recover and begin a cultural and political rebirth. The Aboriginal peoples were the trappers, traders, and scouts for the fur trade, but the result of their effort and expertise on behalf of the great fur companies was the near-destruction of their own society.

C.W. JEFFERYS

THE MÉTIS: A NEW NATION

The fur trade and western exploration also helped create a new nation, the Métis, who were the offspring of European men and Aboriginal women. Relationships between the two societies had a long history in eastern North America. There, Aboriginal peoples were involved with early fishers who came to the East coast, and with the traders and coureurs-de-bois of New France. Champlain had once promised the Aboriginal people:

"Our young men will marry your daughters and we shall be one people."

In the West, English speakers of this new nation were at first called half-breeds. The French were called Métis, meaning mixed. Métis is now the general term for this nation that numbers half a million today.

Telling Their Stories

Lizette Duval, the daughter of a French-Canadian voyageur and an Aboriginal mother, was only 14 years old when she was given as a "country wife" to NWC fur trader Daniel Harmon. View the clip *The Winterer* (Episode 6, *Canada: A People's History*, 40:33 to 45:11). How do you think Lizette Duval viewed her marriage? What role do you think she and other country wives played in the building of Canada? What is significant about Lizette Duval's story?

How did the Métis hunt buffalo? Before the arrival of the horse, the hunters would sneak up on the animals under buffalo pelts or other furs. Sometimes the hunters would rush the animals, making them stampede over cliffs called buffalo jumps. The women slaughtered and cut up the animals. Every part of the buffalo was used: for food, tools, clothing, and shelter. Once they had horses, the Métis organized huge hunts on the Praries, but by the 1880s, the Prairie bison was nearly extinct. A single great herd lives today in Wood Buffalo National Park in Alberta.

THE MÉTIS BUFFALO HUNT

In many ways, the Métis were not really accepted by either the European or the Aboriginal communities. They began to see themselves as a new nation and developed their own culture and identity.

The Métis were vital to the fur trade, because they provided pemmican, a recipe of dried buffalo meat mixed with fat and berries, to the voyageurs. Pemmican was easy to transport and extremely nutritious and it sustained the voyageurs as they canoed along the western waterways and portaged with their back-breaking loads.

The buffalo hunt was the key to the economy and the culture of the Métis. They were superb riders and skilled shooters. Their hunts consisted of long, winding caravans of Red River carts, and were organized under a governor and 10 captains. One participant noted these numbers for a buffalo hunt in 1840:

> *"620 hunters, 650 women, 360 children, 1210 carts with draught animals and 403 hunting horses, 740 guns, 568 litres of gunpowder, 590 kilograms of shot as well as countless flints, knives, hammers and axes."*

Alexander Ross quoted in *Horizon Canada*, number 16 p.369.

Camp Providers, **Alfred J. Miller**

The meat and hides provided food, clothing, and tools for the Métis. The remaining food was then prepared as pemmican and traded.

The arrival of permanent European and Canadian settlers on the prairies threatened the Métis way of life and possession of the land. There were three terrible clashes with the ever increasing newcomers: The Seven Oaks Massacre in 1816, the Riel Rebellion in 1870, and the Northwest Rebellion in 1885. Many lives were lost in this clash of cultures in Canada's West. Today, the Canadian constitution recognizes the Métis as one of Canada's Aboriginal peoples and many Métis have made and are making a unique contribution to Canadian life.

◀ Playback ▶

1. **What impact did European diseases have on Aboriginal peoples?**

2. **Who are the Métis? Briefly describe their way of life when their nation began.**

3. **How did the fur wars impact the Métis?**

4. **Are people of mixed blood more accepted or less accepted in Canada today than the Métis were in past years?**

The Back Story

Different views about issues can be confusing and even frustrating, but they give us the opportunity to get as much information as possible before making a decision.

One heated issue in Canadian history is the impact and nature of the fur trade. It was clearly central to exploration and development in Canada. But it had costs.

The Goal

"Be it resolved that the benefits of the fur trade outweighed the drawbacks." Outline as many arguments as you can both for and against the resolution. When you have listed all of the arguments, choose the position you most agree with. Then write a one-page statement outlining and defending your view.

History in Action
The Great Debate

The Steps

1. Copy the chart shown here into your notebook. Create a list of affirmative and negative arguments about the impact of the fur trade on Canada.
2. You may use both current and historical information. Some questions you might ask yourself are:
   - Was there an alternative way or reason to explore North America?
   - Did the fur trade benefit everyone equally?
   - What was the impact on the environment?
   - Should we celebrate or show disdain for the fur trade?
   - How do you feel about the fur trade today?
3. Choose the position you most agree with.
4. Write a one-page statement outlining and supporting your view.
5. Debate the resolution with a partner or as part of a pair of groups. Have a classmate or your teacher determine the winner.

Evaluating Your Work

These are the criteria you should think about as you complete your work. Your work should:
- Include a neat and carefully completed worksheet
- Show that you have thoughtfully considered all the pro and con arguments before writing your position paper
- Include a clear and well-supported statement of your position
- Be read in a clear, audible voice
- Show your ability to listen to other points of view before responding
- Show your ability to offer brief, focused comments during the debate

Affirmative (Pro) Arguments	Negative (Con) Arguments

CHAPTER 4

EXPLORING CANADA'S RICHES

Voyageurs at Dawn, Frances Ann Hopkins

A s Jacques Cartier had noted hundreds of years before, Canada was a land filled with natural riches. Many men, and a few women, were driven to find those riches and in doing so continued to map and shape the country. The difficult job of merging HBC and the NWC fell to George Simpson, the new governor of HBC. Simpson had learned the business in a small fort on an isolated island in Lake Athabaska. Nicknamed "the Little Emperor," he would dominate the fur trade and the Northwest for 40 years.

George Simpson

Frances Ann Hopkins: Artist of the Northwest

Frances Ann Hopkins was one of the few European women to spend any time on the fur frontier. She captured her experiences in a series of brilliant paintings and drawings that richly share the spirit of the voyageurs and the realities of the fur trade. Hopkins, who lived in Canada from 1858 to 1870, was married to George Simpson's private secretary. The daughter of an Arctic explorer, she had an adventurous spirit and accompanied her husband on many great canoe voyages of the Northwest. Her artistic record has preserved much of the romance of the fur trade.

THE LITTLE EMPEROR

Simpson's first job was uniting two warring groups to serve HBC. He held a party at York Factory, where he was able to bring the former enemies together under his leadership.

The governor earned his nickname by being an uncompromising ruler. Now that two companies were one, HBC needed far fewer posts and employees. Simpson wrote that it was time for "the broom and pruning knife." He began reducing the size of the business and increasing profits with zeal. In a few years, he closed 73 posts and cut the work force by half.

Facing no competition, Simpson drove harder bargains with the Aboriginal traders. The elaborate ceremonies once used to win Aboriginal business were no longer needed, so Simpson ended them. He abandoned the long NWC route from Fort William to Montreal. Furs were sent to the bay and then directly to England. Simpson had large York boats built which could carry huge quantities of furs from posts such as York Factory. Under Simpson, HBC and the fur trade had become less of a risky adventure and more of a modern business.

Simpson acted the role of emperor in his personal life, too. He married, then discarded, several wives. He made many long voyages, but never paddled. Even in the wilderness, he dressed impeccably. A Scottish piper often played in advance of Simpson's arrival. His personal secretary took notes for him on his travels, which included five trips to the Pacific coast and a dozen to HBC headquarters in London, England.

Simpson was knighted in 1841. He retired to Montreal and died there in 1860 a very wealthy, but lonely, man.

THREE WHO EXPLORED A CONTINENT

Much of the later exploration and mapping of the territories of Canada's Northwest was done by three remarkable men: David Thompson, Alexander Mackenzie, and Simon Fraser.

Smart and strong, these men worked with the Aboriginal peoples in a partnership that shaped the future destiny of Canada. On canoe and on foot, they explored where no Europeans had yet been. They came to know the wilderness and opened its secrets to the fur trade and to much later settlement.

As you read their profiles, note what elements seem common to the exploits of each adventurer.

Alexander Mackenzie

Born: Stornaway, Scotland, 1774, **Died:** Dunheld, Scotland, 1820

Alexander Mackenzie settled in New York during the Revolutionary War. He later moved to Montreal where he joined the fur trade and ran a post at Ile à La Crosse. Mackenzie joined the NWC in 1787, working in the Athabaskan region and then building Fort Chipewyan. Soon he began searching for a route to the Pacific Ocean.

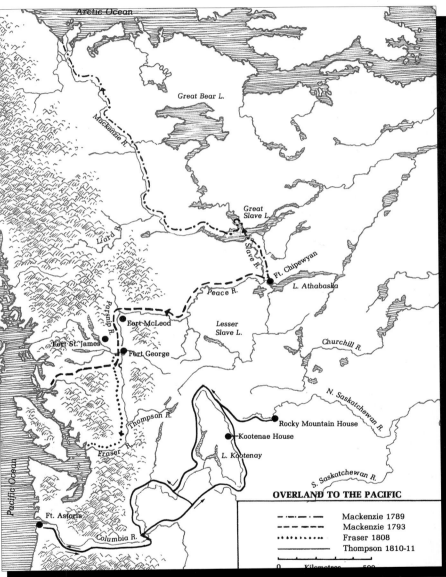

Mackenzie first followed a river out of Great Slave Lake but the ocean he found was the Arctic, not the Pacific. Mackenzie was so bitter, that he called the river "River of Disappointment." The river now bears his name and is one of the great waterways of North America.

Mackenzie returned to England to study and get more surveying equipment. In 1793 he came back to Canada determined to reach the Pacific. Taking easier routes and staying away from unfriendly First Nations, he crossed the Rockies and followed the Bella Coola River to saltwater. He had become the first European to cross the North American continent. He described making a marker of his achievement.

"I now mixed up some vermillion in melted grease, and inscribed in large characters ... this brief memorial: Alexander Mackenzie from Canada, by land. The 22nd of July, one thousand seven hundred and ninety-three."

The exploration and mapping of the vast Northwest was largely the work of three explorers who worked for the NWC. Thompson, Fraser, and Mackenzie lived exciting, challenging lives that shaped a nation.

Mackenzie published an account of his voyages and became an international sensation. He was knighted in 1802 and was elected to the legislature of Lower Canada in 1805. He later

Alexander Mackenzie

Simon Fraser

David Thompson

returned to England, married into a wealthy family, and died a prosperous landowner.

Although his travels were remarkable, he followed difficult routes and rivers that were not of much use for the fur trade. It would be another man who would find an acceptable commercial route to the Pacific.

Simon Fraser
Born: Mapleton, Vermont, 1776. **Died:** St. Andrews, Canada, 1862

The son of a Loyalist officer (Loyalists were those in British North America who stayed loyal to Britain), Fraser came to Canada from Vermont. He joined the NWC as a clerk and by 1799 was working in the fur-rich Athabaska region of the Northwest. By 1801, he had become a partner. In his work for the NWC, Fraser spent years exploring the lands west of the Rockies. He established a string of fur trading posts, including Prince George. He looked for the Columbia River but failed to find it. He travelled part of the way through the dangerous canyon of the current-day Fraser River (named in his honour by David Thompson.) In 1815, he returned to the Athabaska region to oversee its fur trade for the NWC.

David Thompson
Born: Born: London, England, 1770. **Died:** Longueuil, Canada, 1857

In 1784, a 14-year-old orphan named David Thompson was purchased by HBC for $15.00. He would become a great North American mapmaker and a geographer of the fur trade. He longed to leave the small HBC post and explore the interior. While recuperating from a broken leg, he studied under an experienced HBC surveyor and soon became skilled himself at surveying and map-making. When in the presence of local Aboriginals, he listened closely to their wisdom and lore.

> *Every day we passed from 12 to 15 polar bears, lying on the marsh, a short distance from the shore...The Indian rule is to walk past them with a steady step without seeming to notice them.*

HBC rewarded the smart young man with his own set of surveying instruments and in 1792, sent him to find a new, shorter route to the Lake Athabaska region, which he did successfully.

In 1797, HBC ordered Thompson to stop surveying and come back to the Bay. Instead, Thompson walked 80 miles in the snow to the nearest NWC trading post. There he was hired, given more money, and encouraged to keep exploring. Before long Thompson's endless curiosity and energy had helped complete the mapping of the fur trade routes east of the Rockies. In 1806 he was sent off on a grand adventure to find a way to the Pacific. Carefully working with local First Nations and avoiding conflict, Thompson discovered the Athabaska Pass route through the Rockies and reached salt water by travelling down the great Columbia River to the Pacific. By the time he retired in 1812, he had surveyed 3 500 000 square kilometres of Canadian wilderness. He created the first real map of the Northwest. Most explorers and traders created only rough sketches, but Thompson's maps were works of art and science. Sadly, no one was interested in publishing even part of Thompson's 77 remarkable travel journals. He died poor and blind in almost as humble a position as he began.

View the clips *Looking at Stars* (Episode 6, 45:13 to 48:43) and *The Columbia* (Episode 6, Hour 2, 0:00 to 15:00) from *Canada: A People's History*. What were Thompson's character traits? How did these traits affect how he did his job?

◀ Playback ▶

1. **What steps did Governor Simpson take to remodel the newly merged HBC and NWC?**

2. **Which of his actions do you support? Which of his actions do you not support? Why?**

3. **In your view, who was the greatest of the western explorers: Mackenzie, Fraser, or Thompson? Explain your choice.**

4. **Explain the significance of Frances Ann Hopkins' art.**

Mackenzie's first view of the Pacific

THE PACIFIC COAST: FURS, GOLD, AND COLONIES

The fur trade changed the Pacific Coast forever. Traders focused on the sea otter pelt after Captain Cook learned of its great value. Later, the explorers of the North West Company opened the interior to trade in other furs. The fur trade was the foundation of many West Coast settlements, but other resources would permanently define those communities.

FURS FROM NEW CALEDONIA

The rich fur-trading region of current-day Central British Columbia was first developed by Simon Fraser. The area, called New Caledonia, was known as the "Siberia of the fur trade" because it was remote and surrounded by mountains. It was also rich in pelts. For several years, HBC ran an efficient fur-trading network there, then opened a more convenient trading post at Fort Langley, in the lower mainland, in 1827. Then gold was discovered in the remote area, and the role of HBC would change forever.

GOLD RUSH!

Finding riches was the dream of many early explorers. They found it in furs, but the fur trade was hard work. Many still dreamed of finding gold, even years after Jacques Cartier's find turned out to be only "fool's gold."

Was there really gold in Canada? There was, and it was first found on the Fraser River in the BC interior in 1858.

The area where gold was found was controlled by HBC. The company ran a network of fur-trading posts there. It also ruled the small settlement in the area, under Governor James Douglas. HBC tried to keep the discovery of gold quiet, but that was impossible. In a single year, the number of Europeans living in the area went from 1000 to over 10 000. The governor didn't want to upset the fur trade, and he worried about losing the land entirely to the thousands of gold-crazed miners coming from south of the border. British authorities were worried, too.

Hordes of miners landed on the West Coast to make their fortunes. Almost overnight, mining towns sprang up. In their hurry to get upriver, miners built poor quality boats and tried to sail up the roaring Fraser. Many lost their lives. Each new gold

When miners struck gold on the Fraser River, new towns, including Barkerville, sprung up almost overnight.

Barker claim

find brought a rush of miners, fights, new towns, fortunes made and lost. Miners moved further and further into the interior, searching for the next big strike. The Fraser River Gold Rush was quickly followed by the Cariboo Gold Rush in the interior of British Columbia. This new frontier was wild. The gold rushes quickly overran Aboriginal communities. Douglas and the HBC system could not control events.

A New Province

The British weren't happy about the arrival of so many Americans. They had already tried to protect their own interests by creating the colony of Victoria, on Vancouver Island, in 1849. The discovery of gold made the British even more worried about losing their land. In 1858 they quickly created the colony of British Columbia and named Douglas its governor. The two colonies united as British Columbia in 1866, and entered confederation in 1871.

Barkerville was one of many boom towns built during the Cariboo Gold Rush. How can you tell from this picture that the town was built almost overnight?

Billy Barker

BARKERVILLE: BC BOOM TOWN

The gold rush wasn't called a "rush" for nothing. Everything about the time was a rush. People hurried to get to the interior of British Columbia before the gold was gone. They risked their lives to race to the gold. Towns sprang up in weeks. These instant communities, called "boom towns," could be lawless and disorganized, but they were lively and they provided shelter and services for the miners. When the gold was gone, the towns died just as quickly as they had been born.

Barkerville was one of the most celebrated boom towns of the time. Located in the province's interior, it was the site of an important gold strike. It was named for Billy Barker, a sailor who discovered a huge gold deposit. Barkerville quickly grew to 10 000 people, and claims to be the home of the first permanent Chinese settlement in Canada. Many Chinese came north from California with American prospectors. About 100 of them worked on the Cariboo Road linking Barkerville to Yale, the first place where prospectors could travel on the Fraser River.

In the 1860s, Barkerville called itself "the gold capital of the world." But in 1868, most of the hastily built town was destroyed in a fire. By 1900, most of the gold was gone and the town was almost forgotten. It was rebuilt as a historical tourist attraction in 1959.

Faces on the Frontier

Many people helped lay the foundations of the future
province of British Columbia. Three of them are profiled here.
What do you think they have in common?

Mifflin Gibbs

Mifflin Gibbs was born in the United States. Because he was Black, he was not allowed to vote. When he heard about the gold rush, he chose to come north. He was a successful merchant in Victoria and was later elected to the town council. Gibbs was active in getting British Columbia to join Confederation. He returned to the US in 1870 and became a successful lawyer and politician.

Matthew Bailie Begbie: "The Hanging Judge"

The first justice of the new colony of British Columbia, Matthew Bailie Begbie had a reputation for giving harsh sentences. In the wild times of the frontier, Begbie worked hard to create respect for the law. He later became Chief Justice of the new province of British Columbia.

Amelia Connolly: Wife of the Governor

Amelia Connolly was the daughter of an HBC trader and a Cree woman. She was 16 when she married James Douglas, the future governor of British Columbia, also of mixed parentage. Connolly had 13 children, and became Lady Douglas when her husband was knighted. Connolly's skill in dealing with other people once saved her husband from injury or possible death in a dispute with First Nations.

Sheepshead Claim, Williams Creek, Cariboo, B.C.

◀ Playback ▶

1. Briefly describe life in New Caledonia.

2. How did the discovery of gold change political life on the West Coast?

3. Does gold still lure people today? How?

4. What evidence is there that people from many cultures were part of British Columbia from an early stage?

5. What products would you "rush" to get today?

The Explorer Interviews

The Back Story

Studying history gives you a chance to imagine what it would have been like to live in the past. If you could meet a famous explorer or pathfinder, what would you ask? How might that person look or talk or act?

The Goal

Work with a partner to prepare and present a three- to five-minute interview with an explorer of your choice. You should include both fact-based and opinion-based questions and present your interview in a lively, natural way.

The Steps

1. Choose an explorer from Canada's past (from the Norse up to the time of Confederation).
2. Review the information from this book about that explorer. Do additional research about the explorer using the library, the Internet, and Episodes 1 and 6 of the video *Canada: A People's History*.
3. Take detailed research notes. Record sources used and keep your notes organized.
4. With your partner, create a range of questions to ask your explorer. Organize them in a logical order. Together, prepare answers to your questions.
5. Decide who will be the interviewer and who will be the subject. Rehearse your interview until it seems natural and effortless.
6. Prepare simple costumes for the interviewer and subject and use props if you wish (paddle, furs, and so on).
7. Present your interview to the class. You might also consider videotaping your presentation. Be prepared to answer questions from the audience.

Evaluating Your Work

These are the criteria you should think about as you complete your work. Your work should:

- Be informative and accurate
- Be well-prepared, run smoothly, and be clearly audible
- Use accurate costumes and props
- Be of the required length
- Be presented maturely

CHAPTER 5

FAST FORWARD

Canadian actor William Shatner's Captain Kirk is a popular symbol of the enduring urge to explore.

It might seem like the days of exploration and pathfinding are long gone. Nothing could be further from the truth. Many of the skills taught to the early explorers and traders by their Aboriginal neighbours are now a part of Canadian culture. Think about it. Millions of Canadians enjoy camping, hiking, canoeing, and orienteering. What were once survival skills in a dangerous land are now recreational activities. The surveying, mapping, and charting of Canada's lands and waters is ongoing too. Today lasers and satellites continue the work done by the astrolabe and compass.

These are the voyages of the Starship Enterprise. *Its five year mission... to boldly go where no man has gone before."*
Opening for *Star Trek* **television series**

TODAY'S EXPLORERS

Are Canadians still exploring? We aren't looking for new fur trade routes, but we are exploring the depths of the ocean and the limits of outer space. Canadians are especially active in exploring the microscopic world of genetic science. Many companies and institutions in Canada are in the forefront of the struggle to defeat terrible diseases such as cancer.

What would you like to change? What would you like to look at more closely? What is out there that you might like to find? If you have an open mind and a good imagination, you can explore anything. The Canadian imagination is alive and well and welcoming new explorers. Maybe you'll be one of them.

"I am an explorer. I adventure into the present. I make startling discoveries.
Marshall McLuhan

Roberta Jamieson

Tak Mak

Hayley Wickenheiser

Take a look at the following photographs. What exploration do you see? How many images do you recognize? Which of today's explorers can you identify? How important for Canada is the urge to explore? How important is that urge for you? In what ways are you already an explorer? Think about these questions. Write, draw, or talk about your answers and see what exploration means to you.

Jeff Adams

Craig Keilburger

How do you think Canada's work in space exploration is like the explorations of such men as Cartier and Thompson? What similar skills and characteristics might an astronaut today have to an explorer or fur trader of the past?

THE FINAL FRONTIER

Is outer space the final frontier? Some people think so. New galaxies are like the unknown lands of the past. Spacecraft often have names that bring to mind the voyages of days gone by, such as *Explorer*, *Voyager*, *Challenger*, and *Discovery*. Canada is active in exploring outer space. Canadians have travelled to space and played a major role in scientific exploration. Like Cartier, Thompson, and the explorers of old, they travel to new places, far from home in search of knowledge and the excitement of discovery.

The Canadian Space Agency oversees Canada's space program. The following are some highlights.

1962 • Canada launches science satellite, *Alouette 1* to become the third country in space after the USSR and the US.

1965 • Canada launches its first commercial communications satellite, *Early Bird*.

1974 • NASA awards contract to design and build a remote manipulation system for the Space Shuttle. This system is later named the Canadarm.

1982 • Success of Canadarm leads the US to invite a Canadian to fly in space.

1983 • Canada selects its first six astronauts.

1984 • Marc Garneau is the first Canadian in outer space.

1985 • The crew of the Space Shuttle *Atlantis* performs an experiment about manufacturing mirrors in space. The experiment was designed by two Canadian high school students from Quebec.
• Canada agrees to participate in the International Space Station Project.

1989 • Creation of Canadian Space Agency.

1992 • Roberta Bondar becomes the first Canadian woman in space.
• Canadian Space Agency searches for second group of astronauts.

1995 • Canadian Chris Hadfield becomes first Canadian to visit Russian space station *Mir*.